E

MW01290265

COOKBOOK

THE EFFORTLESS CHEF SERIES

By
Chef Maggie Chow
Copyright © 2015 by Saxonberg
Associates

Published by
BookSumo, a division of Saxonberg
Associates
http://www.booksumo.com/

A GIFT FROM ME TO YOU...

HASHIMOTO KAZUMA

INFINITE SUSHI
A COMPLETE SET OF SUSHI RECIPES

Send the Book!

I know you like easy cooking. But what about Japanese Sushi?

Join my private reader's club and get a copy of **_Infinite Sushi: A Complete Set of Sushi and Japanese Recipes_** by fellow BookSumo author Hashimoto Kazuma for FREE!

<u>Send the Book!</u>

Enjoy some of the best sushi available!

You will also receive updates about all my new books when they are free. So please show your support.

Also don't forget to like and subscribe on the social networks. I love meeting my readers. Links to all my profiles are below so please click and connect :)

<u>Facebook</u>

<u>Twitter</u>

ABOUT THE AUTHOR.

Maggie Chow is the author and creator of your favorite *Easy Cookbooks* and *The Effortless Chef Series*. Maggie is a lover of all things related to food. Maggie loves nothing more than finding new recipes, trying them out, and then making them her own, by adding or removing ingredients, tweaking cooking times, and anything to make the recipe not only taste better, but be easier to cook!

For a complete listing of all my books please see my author page.

INTRODUCTION

Welcome to *The Effortless Chef Series*!
Thank you for taking the time to
download the *Easy Burrito Cookbook*.
Come take a journey with me into the
delights of easy cooking. The point of
this cookbook and all my cookbooks is to
exemplify the effortless nature of
cooking simply.

In this book we focus on the Burrito.
You will find that even though the
recipes are simple, the taste of the
dishes is quite amazing.

So will you join me in an adventure of
simple cooking? If the answer is yes
(and I hope it is) please consult the table
of contents to find the dishes you are
most interested in. Once you are ready
jump right in and start cooking.

— Chef Maggie Chow

TABLE OF CONTENTS

ANY ISSUES? CONTACT ME

If you find that something important to you is missing from this book please contact me at maggie@booksumo.com.

I will try my best to re-publish a revised copy taking your feedback into consideration and let you know when the book has been revised with you in mind.

:)

— Chef Maggie Chow

NOTICE TO PRINT READERS:

Hey, because you purchased the print version of this book you are entitled to its original digital version for free by Amazon.

So when you have the time, please review your purchases, and download the Kindle version of this book.

You might enjoy consuming this book more in its original digital format.

;)

But, in any case, take care and enjoy reading in whatever format you choose!

LEGAL NOTES

COMMON ABBREVIATIONS

cup(s)	C.
tablespoon	tbsp
teaspoon	tsp
ounce	oz
pound	lb

*All units used are standard American measurements

CHAPTER 1: EASY BURRITO RECIPES

BURRITO I

(WET I)

Ingredients

- 1 lb lean ground beef
- 1/2 C. chopped onion
- 2 cloves garlic, minced
- 1 (14.5 oz.) can diced tomatoes with juice, divided
- 1 tbsp Worcestershire sauce
- 1 1/2 tsps chili powder
- 1 tsp paprika
- 1 tsp dried oregano
- 3/4 tsp ground cumin
- 1/2 tsp ground black pepper
- 2 C. refried beans
- 1/4 tsp ground cumin

- 1 (18 oz.) jar beef gravy
- 1 (10 oz.) can enchilada sauce
- 4 large flour tortillas
- 2 C. shredded Cheddar cheese, divided
- 1 C. sour cream, divided
- 1/4 C. chopped onion, divided
- 1/4 C. chopped tomatoes, divided
- 1 C. chopped lettuce, divided

Directions

- Set your oven to 375 degrees before doing anything else.
- Fry your garlic, half a C. of onions, and beef in hot oil, in a frying pan for 9 mins, until the beef is fully done then crumble it. Remove oil excesses from the meat.
- Add the following to your beef, let it boil for 5 mins: black pepper, 1/2 can diced tomatoes, 3/4 tsp cumin, Worcestershire sauce, oregano, paprika, and chili powder.

16

- Get a saucepan and warm up your refried beans and 1/4 tsp of cumin.
- Get a 2nd saucepan and boil the following: enchilada sauce, half of your diced tomatoes, and beef gravy.
- Simultaneously heat the tortillas in the microwave for 30 secs.
- Make four burritos with the following layers in each tortilla: a fourth of the beef mix, a fourth of the refried beans, and a fourth of the cheddar.
- Fold everything into burritos and layer them with the seam downwards in a casserole dish.
- Before baking coat the burritos with some gravy and one C. of cheddar. Cook in the oven for 20 mins.
- Garnish each burrito with some sauce from the casserole dish, a fourth of a C. of lettuce, a fourth of a C. of sour cream and a fourth of a C. of chopped onion and tomato.

- Enjoy.

Amount per serving (4 total)

Timing Information:

Preparation	Cooking	Total Time
30 m	30 m	1 h

Nutritional Information:

Calories	1191 kcal
Fat	59.3 g
Carbohydrates	103.9g
Protein	59.1 g
Cholesterol	179 mg
Sodium	2551 mg

* Percent Daily Values are based on a 2,000 calorie diet.

Burrito Casserole

(Vegan Approved)

Ingredients

- 3/4 C. white rice
- 1 1/2 C. water
- 1 (12 oz.) package frozen soy burger-style crumbles
- 1 (28 oz.) can whole tomatoes, drained, 1/4 C. juice reserved
- 2 1/2 tsps chili powder
- 1 tsp cumin
- 1 (1.25 oz.) package taco seasoning mix
- 2 (10 inch) burrito-size flour tortillas
- 1 (14.25 oz.) can vegetarian refried beans, divided
- 2 fresh jalapeno peppers - seeded, sliced, and divided
- 1 1/2 C. salsa, divided
- 2 1/2 C. shredded Cheddar cheese, divided

Directions

- Set your oven to 375 degrees before doing anything else. Coat a casserole dish with nonstick spray or oil.
- Get a saucepan and add some water and rice to it. Get the water boiling then set the heat to low and let it cook for 20 mins.
- Stir fry the following in a frying pan for 10 mins: taco seasoning, soy crumbles, cumin, tomato juice, and chili powder.
- Layer the following in your casserole dish: tortilla, jalapeno, 1 C. cheddar, half of your beans, salsa, rice, and soy crumbles. Continue layering until all ingredients are used. Coat everything with 1.5 C. of cheddar.
- Cook in the oven for 16 mins. Enjoy hot.

Amount per serving (8 total)

Timing Information:

Preparation	Cooking	Total Time
20 m	45 m	1 h 5 m

Nutritional Information:

Calories	486 kcal
Fat	18 g
Carbohydrates	35.9g
Protein	50.8 g
Cholesterol	45 mg
Sodium	1807 mg

* Percent Daily Values are based on a 2,000 calorie diet.

BURRITO II

(SHRIMP)

Ingredients

- 2 tbsps vegetable oil
- 1/2 C. chopped onion
- 3/4 C. long-grain white rice
- 3/4 tsp cumin
- 3/4 tsp garlic salt
- 1 1/2 C. chicken broth
- 1/2 C. canned diced tomatoes
- 1 (16 oz.) can refried beans
- 3/4 tsp garlic salt
- 1/2 tsp ground black pepper
- 12 oz. frozen cooked shrimp without tails, thawed
- 2 tsps minced garlic
- 1/2 C. plain yogurt
- 1/2 C. mayonnaise
- 2 tsps pureed chipotle peppers in adobo sauce
- 6 (10 inch) flour tortillas, warmed
- 3 C. shredded Cheddar cheese

- 1/3 C. salsa

Directions

- Get a bowl mix evenly: mayo, chipotle peppers, and yogurt. Place in the frig.
- Fry your onions in veggie oil. Then add in 3/4 tsp of garlic salt and your rice and cumin. Stir fry everything for 5 mins then add in diced tomatoes, and chicken broth.
- Get everything boiling then set the heat to low. Place a lid on the pan. Let the rice cook for 20 mins. Until no liquid remains.
- Heat up your refried beans seasoned with some black pepper and garlic salt (3/4 tsp).
- Get a frying pan hot with some nonstick cooking spray and fry your shrimp and garlic until lightly browned but heated fully.
- Place your tortilla in the microwave for 30 secs to warm it.

Then layer with: a half of a C. of shrimp, a fourth of a C. of cheese, a fourth of a C. of rice, and a fourth of a C. of beans.
- Finally add a tbsp of salsa and chipotle. Then serve rolled.
- Enjoy.

Amount per serving (6 total)

Timing Information:

Preparation	Cooking	Total Time
25 m	15 m	40 m

Nutritional Information:

Calories	866 kcal
Fat	45.9 g
Carbohydrates	73.2g
Protein	39.2 g
Cholesterol	160 mg
Sodium	2042 mg

* Percent Daily Values are based on a 2,000 calorie diet.

BURRITO III

(PIE STYLE)

Ingredients

- 2 lbs ground beef
- 1 onion, chopped
- 2 tsps minced garlic
- 1 (2 oz.) can black olives, sliced
- 1 (4 oz.) can diced green chili peppers
- 1 (10 oz.) can diced tomatoes with green chili peppers
- 1 (16 oz.) jar taco sauce
- 2 (16 oz.) cans refried beans
- 12 (8 inch) flour tortillas
- 9 oz. shredded Colby cheese

Directions

- Set your oven to 350 degrees before doing anything else.

- For 5 mins fry your beef. Then for 5 more mins fry your garlic and onions. Remove any oil excesses.
- Combine in the following with the beef: refried beans, olives, taco sauce, green chili peppers, and tomatoes with peppers.
- Simmer everything for 20 mins over low heat.
- Get a baking dish and create the following layers: beef mixture, tortillas, more beef mix, cheese. Continue until all ingredients used. Final layer should be cheese.
- Cook in the oven for 25 mins.
- Enjoy.

Amount per serving (16 total)

Timing Information:

Preparation	Cooking	Total Time
30 m	30 m	1 h

Nutritional Information:

Calories	432 kcal
Fat	23.9 g
Carbohydrates	33.3g
Protein	19.8 g
Cholesterol	68 mg
Sodium	847 mg

* Percent Daily Values are based on a 2,000 calorie diet.

Burrito IV

(Restaurant Style)

Ingredients

- 1/2 C. uncooked regular white rice
- Juice of 1 medium lime
- 1/3 C. chopped fresh cilantro leaves
- 2 C. shredded deli rotisserie chicken
- 1 (8 oz.) package seasoned black beans
- 1 (11 oz.) package flour tortillas for burritos
- 1 C. pico de gallo salsa
- 1 C. shredded romaine lettuce
- 1/2 C. Mexican sour cream or sour cream

Directions

- Prepare your rice based on the package instructions. Then mix in chicken, cilantro and lime juice. Warm your black beans. Place tortillas in the microwave for 30 secs.
- Layer the following in each tortilla: a fourth of a C. of chicken, beans, lettuce, salsa, and sour cream. Roll into a burrito.
- Enjoy.

Amount per serving (8 total)

Timing Information:

Preparation	Cooking	Total Time
30 m		30 m

Nutritional Information:

Calories	312 kcal
Fat	9.9 g
Carbohydrates	39.8g
Protein	16.3 g
Cholesterol	33 mg
Sodium	614 mg

* Percent Daily Values are based on a 2,000 calorie diet.

BREAKFAST BURRITOS FROM MEXICO

Ingredients

- 1 lb bacon
- 10 eggs
- 1 (16 oz.) can refried beans
- 8 oz. shredded Cheddar cheese
- 10 (10 inch) flour tortillas

Directions

- Fry your bacon in a frying pan. Remove oil excess. For 30 secs warm the tortillas in the microwave.
- Get a pan to heat your refried beans. While the beans are heating cook your eggs in oil.
- Layer each tortilla with the following: 1 eggs, some cheese, 2 pieces of bacon. Shape into a burrito. Enjoy.

Amount per serving (10 total)

Timing Information:

Preparation	Cooking	Total Time
25 m		35 m

Nutritional Information:

Calories	638 kcal
Fat	39.1 g
Carbohydrates	44.9g
Protein	25.6 g
Cholesterol	244 mg
Sodium	1181 mg

* Percent Daily Values are based on a 2,000 calorie diet.

Burrito V

(Turkey)

Ingredients

- 3 C. cooked turkey, cut into bite-size pieces
- 1 C. prepared stuffing
- 1 C. mashed potatoes
- 1 C. leftover gravy
- 2 quarts turkey broth
- 1 large onion, chopped
- 1/4 C. self-rising flour
- 10 (10 inch) flour tortillas
- 1 (8 oz.) package shredded Cheddar cheese
- 3 pickled jalapeno peppers, sliced
- 3 tbsps pickled jalapeno pepper juice
- salt and pepper to taste
- 1 tbsp dried parsley

Directions

- Combine onions, turkey, broth, mashed potatoes, and gravy in a pot and bring everything to boil. Continue boiling until the onion becomes soft.
- Heat your tortillas for 30 mins in the microware. Then put an appropriate amount of turkey mix on each.
- Put some cheese and then more turkey mix.
- Finally add some jalapenos and a bit of jalapeno juice.
- Add some parley and salt.

Amount per serving (10 total)

Timing Information:

Preparation	Cooking	Total Time
30 m	45 m	1 h 15 m

Nutritional Information:

Calories	516 kcal
Fat	15.3 g
Carbohydrates	54.2g
Protein	27.7 g
Cholesterol	59 mg
Sodium	1501 mg

* Percent Daily Values are based on a 2,000 calorie diet.

Burrito VI

(Easy American Cheese)

Ingredients

- 1 (10 inch) flour tortilla
- 1/4 C. vegetarian refried beans
- 1 slice American cheese
- 1 pinch ground black pepper
- 1 tsp low-fat sour cream
- 1 dash hot pepper sauce

Directions

- For five mins warm your refried beans.
- Then warm your tortillas in the microwave for 30 secs.
- Layer beans into the tortilla then some sour cream then cheese, and some pepper.
- Finally add some hot sauce.
- Form everything into a burrito.

- Enjoy.

Amount per serving (1 total)

Timing Information:

Preparation	Cooking	Total Time
15 m	20 m	1 hr

Nutritional Information:

Calories	400 kcal
Fat	10 g
Carbohydrates	49.9g
Protein	15.8 g
Cholesterol	29 mg
Sodium	1075 mg

* Percent Daily Values are based on a 2,000 calorie diet.

Burrito VII

(Cabbage and Cheddar)

Ingredients

- 1 1/2 lbs ground round
- 1/2 medium head cabbage, chopped
- 1 1/2 onion, chopped
- 1 tbsp minced garlic
- 1 tsp crushed red pepper flakes
- 1 tsp ground black pepper
- 1 C. water
- 8 (10 inch) flour tortillas
- 2 C. shredded Cheddar cheese

Directions

- Fry your beef in hot oil. Once is it is fully cooked crumble it. Remove any oil excesses from the pan then add in the following: water, cabbage, black pepper, onion, red pepper flakes, and garlic.

- Stir fry for 11 min until all water is gone.
- Warm the tortillas in another pan for a few secs.
- With a spoon fill each tortilla with some meat. Than top the meat with one fourth a C. of cheddar.
- Roll into a burrito.
- Continue for all remaining tortillas and meat.
- Enjoy.

Amount per serving (8 total)

Timing Information:

Preparation	Cooking	Total Time
20 m	25 m	45 m

Nutritional Information:

Calories	448 kcal
Fat	19.3 g
Carbohydrates	44.3g
Protein	24 g
Cholesterol	58 mg
Sodium	647 mg

* Percent Daily Values are based on a 2,000 calorie diet.

Burrito VIII

(Squash and Tomatoes)

Ingredients

- 1 tbsp olive oil
- 1/2 onion, chopped
- 3 small summer squash, sliced
- salt to taste
- 4 (7 inch) flour tortillas
- 1/2 C. shredded Cheddar cheese
- 1/2 C. chopped tomato

Directions

- Fry your onion in olive oil for 4 mins. Then mix in one third of your squash let it get soft.
- Then add another third. Let it get soft. Then add the last of it.
- Add some salt for seasoning.
- For 10 sec microwave your tortillas.

- Then fill each one with some spoonfuls of squash.
- Then layer some tomatoes and cheddar. Form a burrito and enjoy.

Amount per serving (2 total)

Timing Information:

Preparation	Cooking	Total Time
15 m	10 m	25 m

Nutritional Information:

Calories	478 kcal
Fat	24.1 g
Carbohydrates	49.7g
Protein	17.6 g
Cholesterol	36 mg
Sodium	865 mg

* Percent Daily Values are based on a 2,000 calorie diet.

Burrito IX

(Rice and Beans)

Ingredients

- 1 C. white rice
- 2 C. water
- 1 tbsp butter
- 1/2 sweet yellow onion, chopped
- 2 cloves garlic, minced
- 1 tbsp butter
- 1 tbsp chili powder, or more to taste
- 1 tbsp paprika
- 1 tsp ground cumin
- 1 tsp freshly cracked black pepper
- 1 tsp cayenne pepper
- 1/4 tsp ground cloves
- 1/4 tsp freshly ground nutmeg
- 1 (15 oz.) can black beans, drained
- 1 (8 oz.) can tomato sauce
- 8 large flour tortillas, warmed
- 2 tbsps chopped fresh cilantro

Directions

- Add some water and rice to a pot and heat it until boiling. Then lower the heat and let it simmer with a lid for 25 mins until the rice is soft.
- Fry your onions and garlic in 1 tbsp of butter for 7 mins. Then add another tbsp of butter then add in chili powder, cloves, paprika, nutmeg, cumin, cayenne, and black pepper, and cook for another 3 mins.
- Make sure you stir fry these onions and seasonings continually so burning occurs.
- Add in your beans and tomato sauce and heat until lightly boiling then set the heat to low and cook for 11 mins.
- Turn off the heat and add in your cilantro and let everything sit for 6 mins.

- To make burritos: fill each tortilla with one third bean mix, and a half of a C. of cooked rice.
- Enjoy.

Amount per serving (8 total)

Timing Information:

Preparation	Cooking	Total Time
30 m	20 m	50 m

Nutritional Information:

Calories	428 kcal
Fat	9.9 g
Carbohydrates	72.5g
Protein	12.4 g
Cholesterol	8 mg
Sodium	895 mg

* Percent Daily Values are based on a 2,000 calorie diet.

Burrito X

(Wet II)

Ingredients

- 1 lb ground beef
- 1/2 C. chopped onion
- 1 clove garlic, minced
- 1/2 tsp cumin
- 1/4 tsp salt
- 1/8 tsp pepper
- 1 (4.5 oz.) can diced green chili peppers
- 1 (16 oz.) can refried beans
- 1 (15 oz.) can chili without beans
- 1 (10.75 oz.) can condensed tomato soup
- 1 (10 oz.) can enchilada sauce
- 6 (12 inch) flour tortillas, warmed
- 2 C. shredded lettuce
- 1 C. chopped tomatoes
- 2 C. shredded Mexican blend cheese
- 1/2 C. chopped green onions

Directions

- Fry your beef in a frying pan until fully done and then crumble it. Remove oil excesses and then mix in onions.
- Continue cooking them until the onions are see-through. Season everything with the following: pepper, garlic, cumin, and salt.
- Mix in your refried beans and add some green chilies. Heat until the beans are warm then shut off the heat.
- Get a saucepan and add enchilada sauce, chili without beans, and tomato soup. Heat everything until warm.
- Put your tortillas in the microwave for 20 secs to warm them. Then add half a C. of beef, then some lettuce, and then tomato. Form a burrito. Then coat the top with your wet sauce. Finally add some cheese and then onions.

- Melt the cheese in the microwave for about 40 secs. And finish forming the other burritos.
- Enjoy.

Amount per serving (6 total)

Timing Information:

Preparation	Cooking	Total Time
15 m	30 m	45 m

Nutritional Information:

Calories	916 kcal
Fat	42 g
Carbohydrates	92g
Protein	43.9 g
Cholesterol	122 mg
Sodium	2285 mg

* Percent Daily Values are based on a 2,000 calorie diet.

Burrito XI

(Roast Beef)

Ingredients

- 1 tbsp vegetable oil
- 1 onion, chopped
- 1 clove garlic, minced
- 4 tomatoes, chopped
- 2 C. chopped cooked roast beef
- 1 (8 oz.) jar prepared taco sauce
- 1 (4 oz.) can diced green chile peppers
- 1/2 tsp cumin
- 1/8 tsp red pepper flakes, or to taste (optional)
- 6 (7 inch) flour tortillas, warmed
- 1 1/2 C. shredded Cheddar cheese
- 2 C. shredded lettuce

Directions

- Fry your onions and garlic in oil. For about 6 mins. Then combine in your roast beef, chili peppers, red pepper flakes, tomatoes, taco sauce, and cumin. Get the contents to a boiling state then lower the heat so that everything is lightly simmering. Continue to let everything simmer for 27 mins.
- Put two thirds of a C. of beef in each tortilla then add some lettuce and cheese. Form into a burrito. Continue for all tortillas.

Amount per serving (6 total)

Timing Information:

Preparation	Cooking	Total Time
20 m	30 m	50 m

Nutritional Information:

Calories	405 kcal
Fat	18.5 g
Carbohydrates	38.2g
Protein	21.9 g
Cholesterol	54 mg
Sodium	1267 mg

* Percent Daily Values are based on a 2,000 calorie diet.

BURRITO XII

(SAUSAGE)

Ingredients

- 12 eggs
- 2/3 C. milk
- 1/2 tsp salt
- 2 tbsps butter
- 1 lb bulk pork sausage
- 2 tbsps minced garlic
- 1/2 red onion, diced
- 1 tomato, diced
- 1/4 C. chopped fresh cilantro
- 1 (3.5 oz.) can diced jalapenos (optional)
- 1 (1 oz.) package taco seasoning
- 1 1/2 C. shredded Cheddar cheese
- 20 (6 inch) flour tortillas

Directions

- Get a bowl evenly combine: salt, milk, and eggs.
- Fry your eggs in melted butter for 6 mins. Then dice up these eggs and put them in a bowl.
- Fry your garlic and sausage for 6 mins then mix in the onions and continue stir frying until the onions are see-through and the beef can be crumbled. Remove any oil excesses.
- Now combine with the eggs your sausage and also add in: jalapeno, tomato, taco seasoning, and cilantro. Finally add in your cheddar.
- Fill each of your tortillas with the sausage mixture. Then form burritos. Place each burrito in the microwave for 5 mins.
- Enjoy.

Amount per serving (20 total)

Timing Information:

Preparation	Cooking	Total Time
50 m	15 m	1 h 5 m

Nutritional Information:

Calories	296 kcal
Fat	18.8 g
Carbohydrates	19.4g
Protein	11.7 g
Cholesterol	140 mg
Sodium	707 mg

* Percent Daily Values are based on a 2,000 calorie diet.

BURRITO XIII

(KOREAN STYLE)

Ingredients

Meat:

- 6 cloves garlic, minced
- 2 tbsps Korean chile paste (gochujang)
- 1 tbsp soy sauce
- 2 tsps white sugar
- 1 tsp sesame oil
- 2 (10 oz.) cans chicken chunks, drained

Else:

- 4 (10 inch) flour tortillas
- 2 tbsps vegetable oil
- 2 tsps butter, softened (optional)
- 1 C. fresh cilantro leaves

- 1/2 C. chopped kimchi, squeezed dry (optional)
- 2 tbsps shredded sharp Cheddar cheese
- 1 tbsp salsa

Directions

- Set your oven to 350 degrees before doing anything else.
- Get a bowl, and evenly mix the following: sesame oil, garlic, chicken, sugar, soy sauce, and chili paste.
- For 11 mins cover your tortillas in foil and enter then in the oven.
- For 12 min cook your chicken and its associated sauce until the chicken is fully done and the sauce becomes thick.
- Coat each tortilla with half a tsp of butter then top with an equal amount of chicken. Layer on top of the chicken the following, in any order: salsa, cilantro, cheddar, and kimchi.

- Shape everything into burritos.
- Enjoy.

Amount per serving (4 total)

Timing Information:

Preparation	Cooking	Total Time
15 m	15 m	30 m

Nutritional Information:

Calories	597 kcal
Fat	29.1 g
Carbohydrates	45.6g
Protein	38.5 g
Cholesterol	97 mg
Sodium	1635 mg

* Percent Daily Values are based on a 2,000 calorie diet.

Burrito XIV

(Honey and Rice)

Ingredients

- 1 1/2 C. cooked yellow rice
- 1 serving cooking spray
- 8 (8 inch) flour tortillas
- 1/4 C. prepared yellow mustard
- 1/4 C. sour cream
- 1/3 C. honey
- 1/2 C. diced red bell pepper
- 1/2 C. diced green bell pepper
- 1 (15 oz.) can garbanzo beans, drained
- 1 (15 oz.) can black beans, rinsed and drained
- 1 C. corn kernels
- 2 C. shredded cooked chicken
- 1/2 C. shredded mozzarella cheese
- 1/2 C. shredded Cheddar cheese
- 1 1/2 tsps ground cumin
- 1 tbsp honey

Directions

- Coat a casserole dish with nonstick spray. Set your oven to 375 degrees before doing anything else.
- Cook your rice according to the box and set aside 1 and a half C. of it. Store the rest in the fridge or freezer for another time or recipe.
- Get a bowl, mix the following: one third C. of honey, mustard, and sour cream. Set aside.
- Get a 2nd bowl, mix: corn, red and green peppers, black beans, and garbanzo beans. Set aside one half a C. of this mix.
- Layer the bottom of your casserole dish with four tortillas.
- Add the following to your beans as a filling for the burritos: honey sauce, chicken, yellow rice, one fourth mozzarella, cumin, and one fourth cheddar.

- Enter the new mix into your casserole dish and layer 4 more tortillas on top. Layer all the remaining cheese on top and the half of a C. of bean mix set aside earlier.
- Enter the casserole dish into the oven for 45 mins covered with some foil.
- Garnish with two tbsps of honey.
- Enjoy.

Amount per serving (8 total)

Timing Information:

Preparation	Cooking	Total Time
15 m	1 h 5 m	1 h 20 m

Nutritional Information:

Calories	446 kcal
Fat	12.5 g
Carbohydrates	63.2g
Protein	21.4 g
Cholesterol	44 mg
Sodium	602 mg

* Percent Daily Values are based on a 2,000 calorie diet.

Burrito XV

(Pork)

Ingredients

- 3 lbs bone-in pork shoulder roast
- 1 onion, sliced
- 6 cloves garlic, chopped
- 1 (1.25 oz.) package taco seasoning mix
- 6 C. water, or as needed to cover
- 1 (14.5 oz.) can diced tomatoes
- 1 (16 oz.) can refried beans
- 1 (4 oz.) can chopped green chilies, or to taste
- 1 (1.25 oz.) package taco seasoning mix
- 1 (16 oz.) package shredded Cheddar cheese
- 20 (10 inch) flour tortillas
- 1/4 C. vegetable oil, divided

Directions

- Get a big saucepan and bring the following to boil, then let it simmer for 3 hours on low heat, covered: 1 pack of taco seasoning, pork shoulder, garlic, and onions. (Use enough water to cover the pork).
- After 50 mins of boiling add some more water if everything has evaporated. Set aside 1 C. of this liquid after the boiling time has elapsed.
- Shred your pork and discard any fat or bones. Add to your pork the following: remaining pack of taco mix, tomatoes, reserved liquid, green chilies, and refried beans.
- Fill each tortilla with this mix then add some cheddar. Roll each into a burrito. Fry the burritos for 3 mins per side in some hot veggie oil. Then layer them on paper towel to remove oil excess.
- Enjoy.

Amount per serving (20 total)

Timing Information:

Preparation	Cooking	Total Time
30 m	2 h 30 m	3 h

Nutritional Information:

Calories	462 kcal
Fat	22.2 g
Carbohydrates	43.9g
Protein	19.9 g
Cholesterol	52 mg
Sodium	1028 mg

* Percent Daily Values are based on a 2,000 calorie diet.

Burrito XVI

(Avocado)

Ingredients

- 1 tbsp butter, divided
- 1 C. diced red potatoes
- 1 1/2 C. chopped onion
- 6 eggs, beaten
- salt and ground black pepper to taste
- 8 (7 inch) whole wheat tortillas
- 1 lb cooked and crumbled turkey bacon
- 1 1/2 C. shredded low-fat Cheddar cheese
- 1 large avocado, thinly sliced
- 1/2 C. salsa, or as needed
- 1/2 C. reduced-fat sour cream, or as needed

Directions

- For 16 mins stir fry your potatoes in 1.5 tbsps of hot butter. Then place them in a bowl.
- Melt the rest of the butter and fry your onions for 12 mins. Then place them in a bowl too.
- Get another bowl, and evenly mix: pepper, eggs, and salt together.
- Cook these eggs for 5 mins with medium heat.
- On each of your tortillas put some potato mix, salsa, eggs, sour cream, onions, avocado, cheddar, and bacon.
- Shape everything into burritos.
- Enjoy.

Amount per serving (8 total)

Timing Information:

Preparation	Cooking	Total Time
20 m	20 m	40 m

Nutritional Information:

Calories	439 kcal
Fat	25.8 g
Carbohydrates	36.1g
Protein	24.1 g
Cholesterol	205 mg
Sodium	1194 mg

* Percent Daily Values are based on a 2,000 calorie diet.

Burrito XVII

(Creamy Mushroom)

Ingredients

- 1 lb ground beef
- 1/2 yellow onion, chopped
- 1 (14 oz.) can refried beans
- 1 C. shredded sharp Cheddar cheese
- 1 (1 oz.) package taco seasoning
- 6 (9 inch) flour tortillas
- 1 (10.75 oz.) can condensed cream of mushroom soup
- 8 oz. sour cream
- 1/2 C. salsa, or to taste (optional)
- 1 1/2 C. shredded sharp Cheddar cheese

Directions

- Set your oven to 350 degrees before doing anything else.

- For 11 mins fry your beef and onions in oil. Remove any oil excesses. Mix in taco seasoning, refried beans, and 1 C. of cheddar.
- Get a bowl, mix: salsa, sour cream, and mushroom soup.
- Fill each tortilla with an equal part of ground beef. Then shape them into burritos.
- Layer half of the mushroom mix in the bottom of a casserole dish. Then layer your burritos on top of the mushroom mix.
- Coat the burritos with the remaining mushroom mix.
- Add 1.5 C. of cheddar as the final layer.
- Cook in the oven for 36 mins.
- Enjoy.

Amount per serving (6 total)

Timing Information:

Preparation	Cooking	Total Time
15 m	40 m	55 m

Nutritional Information:

Calories	745 kcal
Fat	43.7 g
Carbohydrates	51.9g
Protein	35.2 g
Cholesterol	118 mg
Sodium	1724 mg

* Percent Daily Values are based on a 2,000 calorie diet.

Burrito XVIII

(Chorizo)

Ingredients

- cooking spray
- 3/4 lb chorizo sausage, casings removed and crumbled
- 1/2 C. chopped red onion
- 1 green chili pepper, seeded and diced
- 4 eggs
- 4 flour tortillas
- 1 C. shredded Cheddar cheese

Directions

- Get a bowl and beat your eggs in it.
- Fry your chorizo in a pan coated with nonstick spray until fully cooked and crumbly.

- Then add to the chorizo, some chili pepper, and onions. Continue stir frying until the onions are soft. Add in your eggs and scramble them.
- Put your tortillas in the microwave for 20 secs to warm them.
- Then fill each tortilla with an even amount of chorizo and egg mix. Shape everything into burritos.
- Enjoy.

Amount per serving (4 total)

Timing Information:

Preparation	Cooking	Total Time
15 m	15 m	30 m

Nutritional Information:

Calories	822 kcal
Fat	53.7 g
Carbohydrates	43g
Protein	39.5 g
Cholesterol	243 mg
Sodium	1760 mg

* Percent Daily Values are based on a 2,000 calorie diet.

BURRITO XIX

(SPINACH)

Ingredients

- 2 tbsps olive oil
- 1 C. diced onion
- 3 cloves garlic, minced
- 2 tbsps chili powder, or to taste
- 1 tsp ground cumin
- 1/4 C. water
- 4 C. chopped fresh tomatoes
- 1 (15 oz.) can kidney beans, drained and rinsed
- salt to taste
- 1 (10 oz.) package frozen chopped spinach, thawed and drained
- 4 (10 inch) flour tortillas
- 1 ripe avocado, sliced
- 4 tbsps sour cream
- 4 tbsps salsa

Directions

- Fry your onions and garlic for 6 mins in hot oil. Then add in your cumin and chili powder. Cook for another 2 mins. Add in your salt, water, kidney beans, and tomatoes. Get everything boiling then lower the heat and let it simmer for 22 mins.
- Add in your spinach and let it cook about 6 more mins.
- Put your tortillas in the microwave for 20 secs to warm them.
- Then put an even part of bean mixture in each.
- Form the tortillas into burritos, and top them with salsa, avocado, and sour cream.

Amount per serving (4 total)

Timing Information:

Preparation	Cooking	Total Time
10 m	25 m	35 m

Nutritional Information:

Calories	684 kcal
Fat	29.2 g
Carbohydrates	92.1g
Protein	20.6 g
Cholesterol	6 mg
Sodium	1707 mg

* Percent Daily Values are based on a 2,000 calorie diet.

Burrito XX

(Brown Rice)

Ingredients

- 2 C. cooked Brown Rice
- 1/4 C. salsa
- 1/2 C. cooked, diced chicken
- 1/4 C. shredded Cheddar cheese
- 2 whole wheat tortillas
- 1/4 C. chopped fresh cilantro leaves (optional)
- 2 tbsps sour cream (optional)

Directions

- Get a bowl, and mix: chicken and salsa.
- Microwave the chicken and salsa for 1 min on the highest setting. Then add in your rice and cheese.

- Divide the rice and chicken evenly on your tortillas, then form them into burritos.
- Garnish each burrito with some sour cream and cilantro.
- Enjoy.

Amount per serving (2 total)

Timing Information:

Preparation	Cooking	Total Time
15 m	20 m	1 hr

Nutritional Information:

Calories	352 kcal
Fat	12.1 g
Carbohydrates	51.3g
Protein	17.4 g
Cholesterol	39 mg
Sodium	612 mg

* Percent Daily Values are based on a 2,000 calorie diet.

Burrito XXI

(Hash Browns)

Ingredients

- 2 C. Idahoan(R) Hash Browns
- 3 eggs, scrambled
- 1 (4 oz.) can roasted diced poblano chilies
- 6 (12 inch) flour tortillas
- 3 green onions, finely chopped
- Soft goat cheese
- Salsa verde

Directions

- Prepare your hash browns according to its instructions. Then you want to make your eggs and scramble them. After the eggs are scrambled add in your poblanos.

- Put your tortillas in the microwave for 20 secs. Then add half a C. of eggs, and half a C. of hash browns.
- Add three scoops of goat cheese and some scallions.
- Shape the tortillas into burritos.
- Continue making tortillas until all ingredients are used up. Garnish the burritos with some green salsa.
- Enjoy.

Amount per serving (6 total)

Timing Information:

Preparation	Cooking	Total Time
15 m	20 m	1 hr

Nutritional Information:

Calories	438 kcal
Fat	13.7 g
Carbohydrates	63g
Protein	14.7 g
Cholesterol	99 mg
Sodium	1083 mg

* Percent Daily Values are based on a 2,000 calorie diet.

Easier Chicken Burrito

Ingredients

- 1 lb skinless boneless chicken breasts
- 2 tsps Butter
- 1 pinch Pinch salt
- 1 pinch Pinch pepper
- 2 C. shredded Cheddar
- 2/3 C. Sour Cream
- 1 C. diced green pepper
- 1/3 C. salsa
- 1/2 C. sliced black olives (optional)
- 1 jalapeno pepper, seeded and minced
- 2 tbsps chopped fresh cilantro
- 4 large flour tortillas

Directions

- Set your oven to 350 degrees before doing anything else.

- Dice your chicken into small cubed like pieces.
- Then fry them in butter for 9 mins until fully done. Add in your preferred amount of pepper and salt. Put everything aside in a bowl.
- Add the following to your chicken: cilantro, half a C. of cheese, jalapeno, sour cream, olives, green pepper, and salsa.
- Fill each tortilla with an equal part of chicken mix and shape everything into burritos. Top with some cheese before cooking them in the oven for 22 mins.
- Enjoy.

Amount per serving (4 total)

Timing Information:

Preparation	Cooking	Total Time
10 m	28 m	38 m

Nutritional Information:

Calories	711 kcal
Fat	37.1 g
Carbohydrates	49.6g
Protein	45.5 g
Cholesterol	147 mg
Sodium	1320 mg

* Percent Daily Values are based on a 2,000 calorie diet.

Burrito XXII

(Pork II)

Ingredients

- 3 lbs pork shoulder roast
- 2 C. salsa
- 1 (12 fluid oz.) can or bottle cola-flavored carbonated beverage
- 2 C. brown sugar
- 1/2 (1.27 oz.) packet fajita seasoning
- 2 tbsps taco seasoning mix
- 1 (7 oz.) can chopped green chilies

Directions

- Add 4 C. of water to your slow cooker and then put in your pork. For 5 hours cook the pork with high heat. Remove all liquid and place the pork on a work surface and divide it into four pieces.

- Put your salsa in the blender and puree it. Add it back to the crock pot then add in also: taco seasoning, cola, green chilies, brown sugar, and fajita seasoning.
- Put the pork pieces back in as well and cook for 3 hours on high.
- Shred your pork and then serve with some warm tortillas.

Amount per serving (12 total)

Timing Information:

Preparation	Cooking	Total Time
30 m	8 h	8 h 30 m

Nutritional Information:

Calories	355 kcal
Fat	14.7 g
Carbohydrates	32.6g
Protein	23 g
Cholesterol	73 mg
Sodium	728 mg

* Percent Daily Values are based on a 2,000 calorie diet.

Burrito XXIII

(Pork Steak)

Ingredients

- 1 tbsp vegetable oil
- 5 pork steaks, cut into strips
- 1 (12 oz.) jar salsa
- 10 (8 inch) flour tortillas
- 1 (8 oz.) container sour cream
- 3 green onions, sliced

Directions

- Fry your pork in hot oil. Until completely cooked then add in your salsa and cook for 7 more mins.
- Microwave your tortillas for 20 secs each until warm then evenly divide your pork amongst the tortillas.

- Form them into burritos and top the burritos with some green onions and sour cream.
- Enjoy.

Amount per serving (10 total)

Timing Information:

Preparation	Cooking	Total Time
10 m	15 m	25 m

Nutritional Information:

Calories	299 kcal
Fat	12.8 g
Carbohydrates	30.6g
Protein	14.9 g
Cholesterol	40 mg
Sodium	468 mg

* Percent Daily Values are based on a 2,000 calorie diet.

A GIFT FROM ME TO YOU...

Send the Book!

I know you like easy cooking. But what about Japanese Sushi?

Join my private reader's club and get a copy of **_Infinite Sushi: A Complete Set of Sushi and Japanese Recipes_** by fellow BookSumo author Hashimoto Kazuma for FREE!

Send the Book!

Enjoy some of the best sushi available!

You will also receive updates about all my new books when they are free. So please show your support.

Also don't forget to like and subscribe on the social networks. I love meeting my readers. Links to all my profiles are below so please click and connect :)

Facebook

Twitter

COME ON...
LET'S BE FRIENDS :)

I adore my readers and love connecting with them socially. Please follow the links below so we can connect on Facebook, Twitter, and Google+.

Facebook

Twitter

I also have a blog that I regularly update for my readers so check it out below.

My Blog

CAN I ASK A FAVOUR?

If you found this book interesting, or have otherwise found any benefit in it. Then may I ask that you post a review of it on Amazon? Nothing excites me more than new reviews, especially reviews which suggest new topics for writing. I do read all reviews and I always factor feedback into my newer works.

So if you are willing to take ten minutes to write what you sincerely thought about this book then please visit our Amazon page and post your opinions.

Again thank you!

INTERESTED IN OTHER EASY COOKBOOKS?

Everything is easy! Check out my Amazon Author page for more great cookbooks:

For a complete listing of all my books please see my author page.

Manufactured by Amazon.ca
Bolton, ON

15278620R00057